LEADERSHIP IN SPORTS

BY JAMES HANCOCK

BLUE OWL
BOOKS

TIPS FOR CAREGIVERS

Leadership can be an intimidating and abstract concept. Finding ways to encourage small, everyday examples of leadership can help instill the traits of a good leader in young readers. It is important to know that there are many leadership traits, forms of leadership, and types of leaders. By helping young people identify all of the possibilities, you can help them find which types of leaders they want to be. Learning how to demonstrate the traits of a leader is a form of social and emotional learning (SEL).

BEFORE READING

Talk to the reader about leadership.

Discuss: What does leadership mean to you?
Who are some leaders in your life? How do they lead?

AFTER READING

Talk to the reader about how he or she can practice leadership.

Discuss: How can you practice different types of leadership while playing sports?

SEL GOAL

Young readers may have a hard time seeing themselves as leaders. Lead students in a discussion about times they have been team players. Discuss the leadership traits in this book. Help them start to identify leadership traits in themselves. Have students think of times they have used these traits in sports or other activities.

TABLE OF CONTENTS

CHAPTER 1
What Is Leadership? 4

CHAPTER 2
Leading On the Field 8

CHAPTER 3
Leading Off the Field 16

GOALS AND TOOLS
Grow with Goals 22
Try This! 22
Glossary 23
To Learn More 23
Index 24

WHAT IS LEADERSHIP?

Coach calls to the team, but no one is listening. Deb hears. She runs to start the huddle. The rest of the team joins. Deb is a leader on the court!

coach

Leadership is the ability to lead others. A leader is someone we want to follow. We look up to leaders for their actions and **traits**. Coaches lead us in sports. They train us and give us direction.

Coaches want us to do well. They show us skills. They **support** us and cheer us on!

Coaches aren't the only leaders in sports. Everyone can be a leader. You probably already are!

LEAD YOURSELF

Not everyone plays a team sport. How can you be a leader in individual sports? You can lead yourself! Be **disciplined**, and work hard. Support other athletes. Help them learn the skills you already know.

CHAPTER 2

LEADING ON THE FIELD

Max leads by example. He works hard and pushes himself. This **motivates** his teammates. They see him working hard. It pushes them to work as hard as Max!

Leaders in sports are team players. Max doesn't get mad when another teammate does as well as him. He supports him! Team players **contribute** to their team and to their sports community.

Team sports aren't about you shining on the field. They are about working together! Share the spotlight with your teammates. Work together to come up with **strategies** that use everyone's best skills.

The score is tied. The game is getting intense! Someone on the **opposing team** falls. It would be easy to walk away, but Lin helps her up. Showing good **sportsmanship** involves supporting others, even when they're not on your team. After the game, Lin starts the high five line with the other team.

STAY POSITIVE

There might be times when you lose or feel like you let your team down. Don't **pout** or be a sore loser. **Focus** on the positive! What did you learn from that game?

Goals are fun to score in sports! But leaders also set **goals** in sports. Setting goals can help you focus. Cole's goal is to master a new trick on his snowboard. He sets goals with his fellow athletes, too! They keep each other focused.

SET GOOD GOALS

Make sure your goal is **achievable**. You probably won't win every time. But you could win more than last season! Make your goal **specific**, too. Then decide when you want to complete it. Is it a goal you can do by tomorrow or by the end of the season?

LEADING OFF THE FIELD

You can be a leader off the field, too. Sal helps other athletes. She shares her skills and talents with people new to tennis.

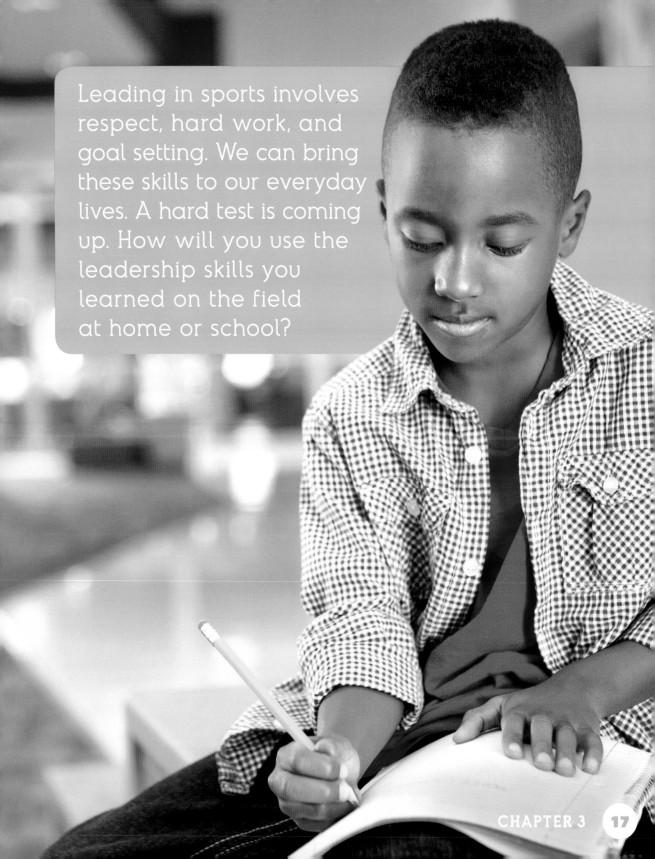

Leading in sports involves respect, hard work, and goal setting. We can bring these skills to our everyday lives. A hard test is coming up. How will you use the leadership skills you learned on the field at home or school?

The crowd cheers. It feels good! We can cheer for our teammates, too. Tell your teammates that you believe in them. Cheer for other players and teams, too! Supporting and **encouraging** others are leadership actions.

WAYS TO ENCOURAGE

Encouragement can be loud, like when we cheer. But it can be quiet, too, with just a smile or a thumbs up. Different people like different kinds of encouragement. Ask your teammates what kind they like.

Being a leader is hard work! But it is **rewarding**. When you are a leader, you can do amazing things. Your team works together to win games. You reach your individual goals. You learn and grow into a better athlete!

GOALS AND TOOLS

GROW WITH GOALS

Leadership takes practice, just like skills in sports. Next time you head down to the court, field, arena, or rink, try one of these goals.

Goal: Choose a way you can lead by example. Is it working hard or having a positive attitude? Pick it out ahead of time. Try to show that leadership trait 5 times during the game or practice. Where else can you show this trait?

Goal: Think of ways that you can show good sportsmanship! How can you be a good sport when you win? How can you be a good sport when you lose? Try doing one of these things the next time you play your sport!

Goal: Encourage others! Find out how your friends like to be encouraged. Maybe you could make a sign for their next match. Or you could help them practice for their next meet.

TRY THIS!

Pick a sports goal you hope to achieve. Maybe you want to master your free throw in basketball or throw a spiral in football. Remember these tips: Make sure your goal is specific and achievable. Then decide when you want to accomplish it. Lastly, write down your goal. Tell a teammate, coach, friend, or parent about it to help you stay focused.

GLOSSARY

achievable
Able to be done successfully after making an effort.

contribute
To give help or ideas in order to accomplish a specific goal.

disciplined
Controlled in behavior.

encouraging
Giving someone confidence, usually by using praise and support.

focus
To concentrate on something.

goals
Things that you aim to do.

motivates
Encourages someone or something to do something or want to do something.

opposing team
The team you play against in a game or competition.

pout
To push out your lips to express annoyance or disappointment.

rewarding
Offering or bringing satisfaction.

specific
Precise, definite, or of a particular kind.

sportsmanship
The way a person or team acts while playing a sport.

strategies
Clever plans for winning.

support
To give help, comfort, or encouragement to someone or something.

traits
Qualities or characteristics that make people different from each other.

TO LEARN MORE

FACT SURFER

Finding more information is as easy as 1, 2, 3.

1. Go to www.factsurfer.com

2. Enter "**leadershipinsports**" into the search box.

3. Choose your cover to see a list of websites.

INDEX

cheer 7, 19

coach 4, 5, 7

community 9

contribute 9

disciplined 7

encouragement 19

focus 12, 15

follow 5

goals 15, 17, 20

huddle 4

individual sports 7

lead 5, 7, 8, 17

motivates 8

opposing team 12

pout 12

respect 17

share 11, 16

skills 7, 11, 16, 17

sportsmanship 12

strategies 11

support 7, 9, 12, 19

team 4, 7, 9, 11, 12, 19, 20

teammates 8, 9, 11, 19

train 5

traits 5

work 7, 8, 11, 17, 20

Blue Owl Books are published by Jump!, 5357 Penn Avenue South, Minneapolis, MN 55419, www.jumplibrary.com

Copyright © 2020 Jump! International copyright reserved in all countries. No part of this book may be reproduced in any form without written permission from the publisher.

Library of Congress Cataloging-in-Publication Data

Names: Hancock, James (Children's writer), author.
Title: Leadership in sports / by James Hancock.
Description: Minneapolis: Jump!, Inc., 2020. | Series: Be a leader | Includes index.
Audience: Ages 7–10 | Audience: Grades 2–3
Identifiers: LCCN 2019039870 (print)
LCCN 2019039871 (ebook)
ISBN 9781645272328 (hardcover)
ISBN 9781645272335 (paperback)
ISBN 9781645272342 (ebook)
Subjects: LCSH: Leadership–Juvenile literature. | Sports–Juvenile literature.
Classification: LCC HM1261 .H36 2020 (print)
LCC HM1261 (ebook) | DDC 303.3/4–dc23
LC record available at https://lccn.loc.gov/2019039870
LC ebook record available at https://lccn.loc.gov/2019039871

Editor: Susanne Bushman
Designer: Molly Ballanger

Photo Credits: Jupiterimages/Getty, cover, 18–19; pat138241/iStock, 1; Duplass/Shutterstock, 3; monkeybusinessimages/iStock, 4; Radius Images/Getty, 5; FatCamera/iStock, 6–7; Mireya Acierto/Getty, 8, 9; Murray Hayward/Alamy, 10–11; SDI Productions/iStock, 12–13, 17; Michael DeYoung/Blend Images/SuperStock, 14–15; Matt Antonino/Shutterstock, 16; isitsharp/iStock, 20–21.

Printed in the United States of America at Corporate Graphics in North Mankato, Minnesota.